NATIONAL AUDUBON SOCIETY
POCKET GUIDES

D1054012

**National Audubon Society**

*The mission of the* NATIONAL AUDUBON SOCIETY *is to conserve and restore natural ecosystems, focusing on birds and other wildlife for the benefit of humanity and the Earth's biological diversity.*

We have nearly 600,000 members and an extensive chapter network, plus a staff of scientists, lobbyists, lawyers, policy analysts, and educators. Through our sanctuaries we manage 150,000 acres of critical habitat.

Our award-winning *Audubon* magazine carries outstanding articles and color photography on wildlife, nature, and the environment. We also publish *American Birds,* an ornithological journal, *Audubon Activist,* a newsjournal, and *Audubon Adventures,* a newsletter reaching 500,000 elementary school students. Our *World of Audubon* television shows air on TBS and public television.

For information about how you can become a member, please write or call the Membership Department at:

NATIONAL AUDUBON SOCIETY
700 Broadway, New York, New York 10003
(212) 979-3000

# FAMILIAR BIRDS OF LAKES AND RIVERS

Text by Richard K. Walton

Alfred A. Knopf, New York

This is a Borzoi Book
Published by Alfred A. Knopf, Inc.

Published in the United States by Alfred A. Knopf, Inc.,
New York, and simultaneously in Canada by Random House
of Canada Limited, Toronto. Distributed by Random
House, Inc., New York.

Prepared and produced by Chanticleer Press, Inc.,
New York.
Printed and bound by Dai Nippon Printing Co., Ltd., Tokyo.

Published February 1994
First Printing

Library of Congress Catalog Number: 93-21252
ISBN: 0-679-74922-5

# Contents

**Introduction**

How to Use This Guide  6
Birdwatching  8
Identifying Birds  12
Birds of the Wetlands  16

**The Birds**  22

**Appendices**

Parts of a Bird  184
Glossary  186
Index  188
Credits  191

## How to Use This Guide

In the pages that follow you will see boldly colored Red-winged Blackbirds, long-legged Great Blue Herons, secretive rails, and many more beautiful and varied birds of North America's lakes and rivers. This guide is designed to help you identify these birds in the field and learn about their habits, life cycles, and history.

Coverage
This guide features 80 species of birds that occur on or near North American lakes, ponds, and rivers. They include swans, geese, and ducks; loons and grebes; wading birds; cranes; marsh birds; shorebirds and gulls; birds of prey; and songbirds. They are presented in the American Ornithologists' Union's taxonomic order.

Organization
There are three parts to this guide: introductory essays; color plates and accompanying descriptions; and appendices.

Introduction
The essay called "Birdwatching" discusses some of the reasons that the pastime is so popular and offers tips on equipment that can enhance the experience. "Identifying Birds" outlines the characteristics you should notice when you look at a bird. Finally, "Birds of the Wetlands" gives specific information about the various types of birds that inhabit our inland waters.

**The Birds** The body of the guide, this section contains photographs of 80 different species of birds in their natural habitats. Facing each photograph is a description of the species, beginning with a short discussion of its unique or unusual traits. The paragraph labeled "Identification" gives a bird's adult size and field marks; its voice, habitat, and range are described in the sections that follow.

Breeding range

Winter range

Permanent range

To supplement the range statement, there is a map on which breeding and winter ranges are indicated by diagonal hatching. Where there is an overlap, or wherever a species occurs year-round, both ranges are superimposed.

Accompanying each species account is a small silhouette, designed as an aid in identification. These silhouettes represent general body types but do not necessarily indicate the subtle variations that can occur among species of the same family.

**Appendices** Following the photographs are a drawing of a wetland bird and another of a wing, labelled with the terms used to describe field marks. The Glossary defines additional terms that may be unfamiliar. Finally, the Index lists both scientific and common names of the species shown.

## Birdwatching

Birdwatching is a fast-growing and enormously popular pastime. Estimates suggest that between 60 and 80 million people are involved with "birding" to some extent. Many of these enthusiasts are backyard birdwatchers, who enjoy feeding their feathered neighbors in return for the opportunity to observe the colorful diversity of local bird life throughout the year. At the other end of the birdwatching spectrum are those whose birding takes them far afield. These birders travel regularly to regional parks and conservation areas and, when time and finances allow, to birding "hot spots" throughout North America. Many birders join in organized bird walks, censusing projects, and fund-raising activities for their local conservation organizations. Typical of this group are the more than 42,000 birders who participate in over 2,000 National Audubon Society–Leica Christmas Bird Counts and National Audubon Society Birdathons, held annually throughout North America. Even more people enjoy birds as a complement to other activities, such as gardening, hiking, jogging, boating, and fishing.

Why do so many people watch birds? There may be as many answers to this question as there are birders. In general, however, birds are diverse, colorful, readily observable, and reasonably easy to identify. Another important attraction may be the relative simplicity of birding. Once you are equipped with a bird guide and binoculars, you are ready to begin. Yet this simple beginning may contain the seeds of a lifelong passion. Whatever direction your new-found interest takes, it won't be long before you can enjoy at least a familiarity with the common species in your area.

Binoculars    A decent pair of binoculars will make birdwatching enjoyable, while binoculars that have poor optics or are damaged will make birdwatching frustrating and even painful. If you already own binoculars, you should "field test" them to see if they are suitable for observing birds. Check the binoculars for clarity of image and ease of focus. Problems may include multiple images, difficult focusing, and image distortion. Essentially, your binoculars should be easy to focus and offer comfortable viewing; eyestrain may indicate that the optics are poor or damaged.

While some beginning birders may be fortunate enough to own a good pair of binoculars, others will want to invest the time and money it takes to learn about and purchase a good pair. There are books on how to buy binoculars, and you may wish to consult one, but a few basic facts will get you started. Specifications for binoculars are stated in a form that includes two numerals separated by a multiplication sign: for example, $7 \times 35$. The first numeral refers to overall magnification; the second, to the diameter (in millimeters) of the objective lens (the lens closest to the object you are observing). So, in this example, the binocular magnifies the image seven times and has an objective lens that is 35 millimeters wide. If you divide the second numeral by the first, the result is what is called the "exit pupil." The exit pupil in this example is 5. This number gives you a relative idea of how much light reaches the eye. A $10 \times 40$ binocular would have an exit pupil of 4, indicating that less light will reach the eye.

Beyond these specifications, comparisons tend to become more difficult. An inexpensive pair of binoculars might have a high exit pupil but poor optics. On the other hand, some excellent binoculars have a relatively low exit pupil but provide a clear, bright image because of their exceptional optics and lens coating. Fine binoculars combine high-quality optics with durable construction.

The old saw "You get what you pay for" definitely applies to the binocular market. At publication, top-grade binoculars cost anywhere from $600 to $1,000. Very acceptable mid-range binoculars, such as several Bausch and Lomb models endorsed by the National Audubon Society, may also be bought for $200 to $500. You may find a good pair of binoculars for less than that, but they are much more likely to have average optics as well as less overall durability. It is wise to shop around, however. For example, one top-rated binocular lists at $1,500 but is widely available for $900.

Spotting Scopes
Certain groups of birds, such as raptors and shorebirds, are better observed with spotting scopes, which are similar to telescopes mounted on tripods. These scopes provide higher magnification than most binoculars; the tripods provide the stability necessary with increased magnification. As is true of binoculars, a wide assortment of scopes is available. Depending on the quality of their optics and housings, prices range between $200 and $1,000. The tripod, an important added consideration, should be chosen for its stability and portability. Avoid spending so much on a scope that you have to settle for a "make-do" tripod. An acceptable scope and tripod will cost about $300 .

**Identifying Birds**

More than a few unfortunate beginning birdwatchers have had the experience of spending time with a seasoned birder who correctly identifies every flitting feather with miraculous ease. Despite outward appearances, the beginner has not witnessed a miracle, and the expert has no superhuman abilities. Consider that time, in the not too distant past, when many teenagers given a fleeting glimpse of a hubcap could correctly identify every automobile in North America. Something similar is going on with the practiced birdwatcher. His or her expertise has developed over time. Given enough time and practice, you can develop the same skills.

Range An important first step in correctly identifying birds is knowing what birds to expect, as well as when and where to expect them. A state bird list, available from your local chapter of the National Audubon Society, will be useful. This Pocket Guide will also help you narrow down the possibilities. Browse through the guide, noting the ranges of the various species, including their seasonal distributions. This will help you to decide if and when a particular species is likely to be in your area. (You may wish to mark pages describing birds that are reasonable to expect in your vicinity.) The Pocket Guide series, because it is organized by types of birds—*Birds of Prey* and *Waterfowl,* for example—allows you to further reduce the possibilities. Your first goal is to know if and when you might expect to see any given bird in your area.

Size   A notion of the overall size of a bird is a critical component of identification. Each species account in this guide includes the body length (from tip of bill to tip of tail) of the bird. Perhaps just as useful are comparative descriptions such as "sparrow-sized" or "crow-sized." Field experience with benchmark species such as the Song Sparrow, American Robin, Blue Jay, American Crow, and Canada Goose will prepare you to use the general sizes of these familiar species in a comparative way to identify unfamiliar birds.

Shape   Some birds can be identified by their shapes alone. In the field, under various light conditions, a silhouette may be all that is discernible. As you gain experience, you will be able to use overall proportions as well as the specific shapes of bills, heads, and tails to confirm a bird's identity.

Color and Pattern   The colorful feathers of many birds are important identifying characteristics. More often than not, however, it is a combination of color and pattern that confirms a bird's identity. In

North America, a robin-sized songbird with an all red head and body, and black wings and tail is a Scarlet Tanager. The Scarlet Tanager is a straightforward example, but the color and pattern of feathers on other species may be quite complicated. In order to deal with this fact, experts use a somewhat specialized vocabulary. Terms such as crown, eye-stripe, eye-ring, and undertail are readily understandable. Other terms, such as mandible, speculum, undertail coverts, and flight feathers, require explanation. To become familiar with what such terms mean, refer to the illustrations and glossary at the back of this guide.

Behavior    Behavioral clues are also useful for identification. Some birds habitually flick their tails, others scratch among the leaves, and still others bob their heads up and down. Some ducks dive and others dabble. There are hawks that hover and hawks that stoop. Some large water birds fly with head and neck outstretched, while others draw in the neck and head. Typical behavior is mentioned in the general description or under "Identification" in each species account.

Voice    Beginners would do well to spend at least some time learning the songs and calls of birds. Virtually all North American birds can be identified by voice alone. Each species account in this Pocket Guide includes a section on "Voice." Both descriptive terms and phonetic clues are given. Start your learning with familiar birds that you hear regularly, and don't be shy about modifying or adding to the ideas given here with your own characterizations of birds' songs. These calls and songs are not only enjoyable to learn, but they can also be very useful in places such as dense woodlands and extensive thickets. A variety of commercial products are available to help you learn bird songs.

Gestalt   Experienced observers use any or all of the clues mentioned above, often in combination with a process of elimination, to identify birds. At times a flick of the tail, a single call note, a flash of color, or a familiar silhouette is enough to confirm an identification. More often a combination of factors reveals the species. At times, birdwatchers refer to the "jizz," or gestalt, of a bird—some overall look or impression that may be difficult to analyze but somehow suggests the given species. Most likely, jizz or gestalt is simply a combination of the various factors outlined here. Ultimately, it is time in the field that will enable you to develop your identification skills.

## Birds of the Wetlands

Visitors to wetlands will encounter a rich diversity of bird life, including loons, herons, waterfowl, shorebirds, gulls, and even a variety of songbirds. This volume focuses on these common wetland birds and includes 80 species from a variety of families. Perhaps the most prominent of wetland birds are the waterfowl. While the more common species are included here, a more comprehensive treatment of ducks, geese, and swans may be found in the *National Audubon Society Pocket Guide to North American Waterfowl.* The *National Audubon Society Pocket Guide to Familiar Birds of Sea and Shore* provides a useful field guide to birders visiting saltwater wetlands.

### Water for Life

Most birds visit water sources daily, whether they are small ponds in city parks, local reservoirs or lakes, or marshy wetlands. These habitats offer food and shelter as well as drinking water. Medium-sized to large bodies of water are also ideal resting places for migratory birds.

### Edges

The diversity of wetland bird life is partly a result of the associated natural resources and partly due to the fact that wetlands create "edges." An edge, or border between two different types of habitats, typically supports a greater diversity of animal life, including birds, than either of the habitats alone. The edges created by wetlands—such as the border between a pond and a cattail marsh—are excellent places in which to concentrate your search for birds. And because bird life in one area will vary seasonally, return trips to the same wetland will be rewarded.

Getting Started   While a pair of binoculars and this guide will get you started, a spotting scope may be useful for observing and identifying birds on large bodies of water. Consult the section called "Birdwatching" for additional tips.

Conservation   The birds of lakes and rivers are among the most vulnerable of all species to human-caused threats. The continuing destruction of wetlands and pollution of their habitats throughout the hemisphere jeopardize the nesting and wintering grounds, as well as migratory stopover points, of countless species. Taking an interest in watching these unique creatures may inspire you to participate in the efforts of the National Audubon Society, and others, to protect bird habitats.

The Families   Birds have been arranged by biologists in groups called families. Knowing the characteristics of the families in this guide will help you to identify the birds you see.

**Water Birds**  Loons (family Gaviidae) and grebes (Podicipedidae) are highly aquatic, diving with ease and swimming expertly underwater, but they are nearly helpless on land. Loons are larger than grebes; they are dagger-billed birds that nest on fresh water in the Far North and winter mostly on salt water. Some grebes are widespread inland all year, even on small marshy ponds. Pelicans (Pelecanidae) are large birds with oddly shaped bills—long and flat, with an expandable pouch to scoop up fish. Cormorants (Phalacrocoracidae) are dark, long-necked, long-tailed birds with webbed feet and hooked bills. They pursue their prey by swimming, often below the surface. Six species of water birds are shown in this guide.

**Wading Birds**  Bitterns, herons, and egrets (Ardeidae) are long-legged, long-necked, spear-billed birds usually seen standing in the shallows waiting to snatch prey. They typically fly with their heads hunched back on their shoulders. Ibises and spoon-bills (Threskiornithidae) are similar, but they fly with their heads and necks outstretched. There are 13 wading birds in this book.

**Waterfowl**  The waterfowl family (Anatidae) includes swans, geese, and ducks. Waterfowl are often sociable and usually migrate in flocks. Geese are often seen feeding on land, and the sexes are similar in appearance. Male ducks, called drakes, are often brightly patterned, while the females (hens) are plain. Dabbling ducks feed with only their heads and foreparts submerged, while diving ducks feed under water. Twelve species of waterfowl appear in this guide.

Birds of Prey  Like all birds of prey, the Osprey, as well as the kites, Bald Eagle, and Northern Harrier (Accipitridae), have hooked bills and powerful talons for hunting. Normally they capture live prey, but the Bald Eagle is also a scavenger and regularly eats carrion. Five birds of prey are shown here.

Marsh Birds  Rails, gallinules, moorhens, and coots (Rallidae) are chicken-like birds often associated with marshes. Rails, gallinules, and moorhens hide in the reeds and grasses and are more often heard than seen. Coots often bob their heads while swimming and are more regularly observed in the open water. The Limpkin (Aramidae) combines the look of a heron with the behavior of a rail. Seven marsh birds appear here.

Cranes  The two species of North American cranes (Gruidae) are closely related to the marsh birds described above. Somewhat resembling our larger herons in overall stature, they differ in flight by having their heads and necks fully extended. Their long, bustle-like feathers are typical, as are their elaborate courtship dances.

Shorebirds and Gulls    Known collectively as shorebirds, the plovers (Charadriidae) and the sandpipers (Scolopacidae) are usually found feeding at the water's edge or in fields. Plovers (Killdeer) are short-billed birds with plaintive voices. Gulls and terns (Laridae) are long-winged, mostly gray-and-white water birds. Most gulls are larger and chunkier than terns. Terns are graceful aerialists with pointed bills and long tails. There are 12 species of shorebirds and gulls in this guide.

Kingfishers    Kingfishers are chunky, large-headed birds with large bills. They nest in burrows and are typically found along streams and at the edges of ponds and lakes. Often they have a favored perch and fish by hovering and diving. Two species of kingfisher appear in this guide.

Songbirds    A variety of songbirds, or perching birds (17 in all), are covered in this volume. Flycatchers (Tyrannidae) are often drab, but the Great Kiskadee is an exception to the rule. Flycatchers usually sally forth from exposed perches to catch insects. Swallows (Hirundinidae) forage in a continuous graceful flight rather than from a perch. They are often seen in small, loose feeding groups in which more than one species is present. Crows (Corvidae) are familiar, large birds with heavy bills. Their diet is omnivorous, and they often call attention to themselves by their raucous vocalizations. The Dipper (Cinclidae) is unique among North American birds and seems to combine the characteristics of a duck and a wren. Wrens (Troglodytidae) are small, hyperactive birds with thin bills and distinctive voices. Some wrens are hole nesters, while others weave complicated grass structures. The American wood warblers (Parulinae) are a diverse and colorful group of small songsters. They feed mainly on insects and are highly migratory. The cardueline finch family (Fringillidae) are generally small and somewhat drably plumaged seed-eaters. They are often found on the ground and migrate in mixed flocks. Lastly, members of the blackbird or troupial family (Icteridae) occur in large flocks during the winter but are normally more solitary on their breeding grounds. They are characterized by sharp-pointed bills and plumages that are either black or a combination of black, orange, and/or yellow.

## Common Loon *Gavia immer*

Loons are large water birds that normally winter along the coast and move inland during the breeding season. The Common Loon seems to prefer isolated lakes, particularly those with numerous bays and islands. Human activities, such as motor-boating, may deter Common Loons from nesting or even cause the parents to abandon their nest. Common Loons are excellent divers and swimmers and rely on a diet of fish.

Identification 28–36". A large black and white bird with a thick bill. In breeding plumage the head is dark green and the back is checkered black and white; there is also a black neck band. In winter birds are basically gray above and white below.

Voice A loud, laughing yodel and a mournful wail, often heard at night on breeding territory.

Habitat Large, forested lakes with many small islands; oceans and bays in winter.

Range Breeds primarily in the North, from Alaska east through northern Canada and in northern forested states. Winters along both coasts and as far south as the Gulf of Mexico.

24

### Pied-billed Grebe  *Podilymbus podiceps*

Grebes are strictly water birds; they rarely set foot on land. A quick inspection of the grebe's anatomy reveals that its legs are set so far back on its body that they are essentially useless for walking on dry land. In its chosen habitat, however, the grebe's leg position and lobed toes move it efficiently on and under the surface of the water. The Pied-billed Grebe, one of the smaller North American grebe species, is named for its two-colored bill, which is apparent during the breeding season.

Identification  12–15". A chunky, plain-looking brown bird with a white rump, invariably seen on the water. It has a pied bill and a black throat in summer and a plain, pale bill and white throat in winter.

Voice  Repeated calls include clucking and hollow cooing: *coo coo coo cuk cuk cuk cuk;* also a nasal whinny.

Habitat  Freshwater ponds, marshes, and sluggish streams; salt water in winter if freshwater habitat is frozen.

Range  Widespread in North America.

## Horned Grebe *Podiceps auritus*

The Horned Grebe, like many other birds, leads a radically different life in summer than in winter. Its outward appearance and its chosen habitat vary greatly with the seasons. During the summer, this gaily feathered bird is strictly a resident of inland, freshwater wetlands. With the arrival of winter, however, the Horned Grebe's plumage takes on a muted character, and the bird abandons its freshwater nesting territories in favor of saltwater coasts.

**Identification** 12–15". A smallish, ducklike bird, invariably found around water. In summer, it shows a rufous foreneck and flanks, as well as golden buff ear tufts. In winter, it is black above and white below, with the white extending up onto the cheek.

**Voice** Loud shrieks, and chatters that sound like a tape recording played on fast-forward.

**Habitat** In summer, lakes and marshes with open water; in winter, mostly on salt water and also on the Great Lakes.

**Range** Breeds from Alaska and northern Canada south to the Great Lakes. Winters along coastal waters.

28

## Western Grebe *Aechmophorus occidentalis*

Two species of grebes that occur mainly in the western United States look so similar that until recently they were considered to be one species. The Western Grebe and Clark's Grebe (*A. clarkii*) both breed on western lakes and winter along the Pacific coast. Both species are well known for their "dancing-on-water" courtship displays. They can be distinguished by their different facial patterns.

Identification  22–29". A large grebe, somewhat resembling a loon. It is overall black and white with a long, thin, yellowish-green bill. The bill in the similar Clark's Grebe is yellowish orange. In the Western Grebe the black head markings extend below the eye, creating a masklike effect. In Clark's Grebe the black cap does not reach the eye.

Voice  A repeated *crick crick!* with the tone like that of a cricket but less measured.

Habitat  Large, freshwater lakes with reeds and rushes for nesting. Winters along coastal shores, bays, and large inland lakes.

Range  Breeds from central Canada south to New Mexico. Winters mainly along the Pacific and Gulf coasts.

30

## American White Pelican *Pelecanus erythrorhynchos*

The American White Pelican is not the bird most people have in mind when pelicans are being discussed. It is the Brown Pelican, a year-round resident of southern coastal areas, that captures its food in spectacular dives into the ocean. American White Pelicans, on the other hand, spend much of the year inland at large, concentrated breeding colonies and do all of their fishing from the surface of the water. They do, however, spend the winter along the southern coasts. These birds are regularly seen circling at great heights.

Identification   54–70". A large, mainly white bird with contrasting black feathers on the wingtips and hind wing. Breeding birds have a massive orange bill with a protruding bulge on the upper mandible.

Voice   Normally silent.

Habitat   Large, inland lakes rich in fish, with islands for nesting.

Range   Scattered throughout inland North America, primarily in prairie provinces and states. Winters in southern California, along the Gulf Coast, and in Florida.

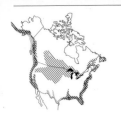

## Double-crested Cormorant *Phalacrocorax auritus*

A cormorant is a large, dark seabird often seen perched on a piling or buoy with its wings outstretched. Cormorants spend much of their time fishing underwater, and this spread-winged pose allows their not-quite-waterproof feathers to dry. Although they have never been domesticated, various species of cormorant have assisted humans. The guano industry in South America is a direct beneficiary of the cormorant, and these birds have been used by fishermen to help catch fish.

Identification 30–36". A large, though slim, long-necked species with an orange throat patch. The thin, hooked bill and the upward tilt of the head are apparent when the bird swims. It often migrates in large numbers in gooselike formations.

Voice Normally silent, except for grunting calls in the breeding colony.

Habitat Lakes, rivers, and rocky coasts; bodies of water that provide plentiful fishing.

Range Widespread in North America. Winters along the coasts, except in the Northeast.

### American Bittern  *Botaurus lentiginosus*

Bitterns are secretive birds that spend much of their time in the tall emergent vegetation that typically surrounds wetlands. The American Bittern's straw-colored feathers provide excellent camouflage, and the bird usually moves in a slow and cautious manner. If it does attract attention, the American Bittern will freeze in place, with bill pointed skyward. Presumably this stance, and the bird's streaked feather pattern, make the bittern resemble its reedy background, providing a further measure of security.

Identification | 23–34". A duck-sized, rather stout bird that is overall tan with some dark streaking and spotting. On the ground, it shows dark "sideburns"; in flight, the dark outer half of the wing is apparent.

Voice | Sounds resembling a stake being pounded into muddy ground, or an old-fashioned water pump: *wonk-a-chunk, wonk-a-chunk.*

Habitat | Heavily reeded fresh- or saltwater marshes and bogs.

Range | Widespread in North America except in the Far North.

## Least Bittern  *Ixobrychus exilis*

One of the challenges of birdwatching is to find those species that seem to make an art of hiding. Most members of the heron family are relatively large, flashy birds that feed in the open and are easy to detect, but the Least Bittern shares none of these characteristics. It is the smallest North American heron, and its size, camouflaging feather colors, and preference for dense wetland vegetation all make the Least Bittern difficult to find. Even in marshy areas, where this bittern is fairly common, the birdwatcher often gets only a brief glimpse.

| | |
|---|---|
| **Identification** | 11–14". A small heron, overall brown, buff, and black. The crown and back are dark (black in males). Perhaps the best field marks are the buff wing patches adjacent to the body. |
| **Voice** | A hollow, rapid *coo-coo-coo-coo.* |
| **Habitat** | Fresh- or saltwater marshes with dense vegetation. |
| **Range** | Primarily east of the Rockies; also southern California. Winters sparingly along the Gulf Coast. |

## Great Blue Heron *Ardea herodias*

Many heron species prefer to nest at coastal locales, but Great Blue Heron rookeries are regularly found inland. A typical heronry, located in the dead trees of a beaver pond, may comprise a dozen or more breeding pairs. Great Blue Herons are adept at catching fish and will stand silently for long periods of time waiting for prey to swim into range. The hunt ends abruptly with a sudden strike from the heron, in which the fish is often impaled on the bird's spearlike bill. After the catch, the "Great Blue" will typically take pains to make sure that the fish is well stunned and in just the right position before swallowing it whole.

Identification    42–52". A large, long-legged, and long-necked bird that often appears dark overall. It has a large yellow bill and, during breeding season, a variety of head and neck plumes.

Voice    Normally silent, but emits a loud, hoarse *craak!* when startled or about to take off.

Habitat    Salt- and freshwater wetlands with tall trees, reeds, or rocky ledges for nesting.

Range    Widespread in North America except the Far North.

### Great Egret *Casmerodius albus*

Common names for birds can be confusing for a number of reasons. Sometimes one bird's name seems to fit another bird. A case in point is the name "Great White Heron." Although this would seem to be an excellent name for the present species, it in fact refers to a white form of the Great Blue Heron. Another source of confusion is changes in names. The Great Egret was formerly referred to as the Common Egret, Great White Egret, and American Egret. The beginner may easily become confused.

**Identification** 37–41". A large white bird with a yellow bill and black legs and feet. Compare with the Snowy Egret (page 44) and the immature Little Blue Heron (page 46).

**Voice** A deep, creaky croak.

**Habitat** Marshes, wooded swamps, and freshwater ponds. Nests in trees or marshy vegetation above the ground.

**Range** Summers from Oregon south to Arizona and along the Gulf Coast, and from the Great Lakes east to Maine and south along the East Coast. Winters along the southeast and Gulf coasts.

### Snowy Egret *Egretta thula*

The Audubon Movement had its beginnings in the late 19th century. The first state organization, the Massachusetts Audubon Society, was established in reaction to the massive plume trade that was devastating southern heron colonies. Thousands of Snowy Egrets, as well as other herons and egrets, were being killed annually to supply feathers to satisfy fashion demands. The conservation movement was begun just in time, and today many heronries are flourishing.

| | |
|---|---|
| Identification | 20–27". A medium-sized egret, largely white with a black bill, black legs, and yellow feet. Compare with the Great Egret (page 42) and immature Little Blue Heron (page 46). |
| Voice | A hoarse croak, similar in tone to a crow's *caw caw caw*. |
| Habitat | Fresh- or saltwater marshes, lakes, ponds, and occasionally cattle fields. |
| Range | Breeds in wetland areas in the western U.S. from Idaho south to Texas, along the Gulf Coast, and in the East from Maine south to Florida. Winters in California and along the Gulf Coast and Florida. |

44

### Little Blue Heron  *Egretta caerulea*

Herons are highly social birds; several species may be found together feeding, in nesting colonies, or at nighttime roosts. The Little Blue Heron is typical in this respect, and its nest is often part of a colony that includes Great Egrets and Snowy Egrets. The Little Blue Heron often feeds along the edges of marshes and ponds but also regularly ventures onto dry land to forage for grasshoppers, crickets, and other insects.

Identification   25–30". A medium-sized, all-dark, slate-gray heron. The adult has gray to black legs, a gray bill with a black tip, and deep purple head and neck feathers. Immature birds are largely white; as they mature, the plumage becomes mottled blue-gray-and-white.

Voice   Normally silent; occasionally croaks or squawks.

Habitat   Freshwater ponds, swamps, and marshes. Nests colonially in trees.

Range   Primarily an inland bird along coastal areas of the southeastern U.S., ranging as far inland as Oklahoma.

### Green Heron *Butorides virescens*

Folk names for birds can be even more confusing than common names. They are often inconsistent from one region to the next; indeed, the same folk name may be used in one area for one bird species and in another region for a different species. However, folk names are often humorous and revealing. The Green Heron is known variously as "fly-up-the-creek," "crab-eater," "swamp squaggin," and "skeeow." Collectively these names tell something of the behavior, diet, habitat, and vocalization of this common heron.

Identification    15–22". A crow-sized, dark heron with short, orange to yellow legs. In good light, the rufous neck feathers and gray-green back are apparent. Young birds are largely brown above and heavily streaked below.

Voice    A short, loud *skeeow,* often heard in flight.

Habitat    Ponds, lakes, streams, and marshes with muddy borders and woodland cover.

Range    Breeds across most of the U.S. Winters in parts of California, southern Arizona, and along the Gulf Coast and Florida.

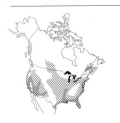

## Black-crowned Night-Heron *Nycticorax nycticorax*

During the daylight hours, Black-crowned Night-Herons occupy a community roost. As dusk approaches, they leave the roost and spend the night feeding in fresh- and salt-water wetlands. In areas where a variety of heron species live, it is sometimes possible to witness a spectacular "changing of the guard," as the night-herons move out to feed and the diurnal herons, such as the Great Egret, Snowy Egret, and Green Heron, return to their roosts.

Identification 23–28". A crow-sized heron, overall black and white with a black crown and back and white underparts. Juveniles are largely brown with white spotting above and brown streaks below. Separating young Black-crowned Night-Herons from young Yellow-crowneds (see page 52) is difficult, but there is heavier white spotting on Black-crowneds.

Voice Flight call is a low, harsh *quawk*, often at dusk or at night.

Habitat Wooded swamps, marshes, and streams.

Range Breeding range is widespread throughout Canada and the U.S. Year-round resident in California, along the Gulf and southeastern coasts, and in Florida.

## Yellow-crowned Night-Heron *Nyctanassa violacea*

Although sometimes found in nocturnal roosts or nesting colonies with Black-crowned Night-Herons, this species is less common. The Yellow-crowned Night-Heron's diet is unusual in that it takes few fish. Crustaceans, including crabs and crayfish, are a mainstay. Like the Black-crowned, this species normally roosts throughout the day and becomes active at dusk.

| | |
|---|---|
| Identification | 22–27". A crow-sized black and gray heron. The creamy white crown has several long plumes in the breeding season. There is a white cheek patch that contrasts with the black face. Young birds resemble young Black-crowned Night-Herons (see page 50). |
| Voice | A harsh, repeated *quawk*, similar to that of the Black-crowned Night-Heron but higher-pitched. |
| Habitat | Wooded river swamps, marshes, and streams, particularly near coasts but also inland. |
| Range | Primarily a southeastern bird, but has been expanding its range from Oklahoma east to Massachusetts. Year-round resident along the Gulf Coast and Florida. |

## White Ibis *Eudocimus albus*

Ibises are closely related to herons and storks. The ibis family comprises 33 different species worldwide. The Latin name for the family, Threskiornithidae, derives from the Greek meaning "sacred bird." The Sacred Ibis was worshiped by the ancient Egyptians, and its mummified remains and carved images are regularly found in the burial vaults of pyramids. The White Ibis, like the other members of the family, is gregarious and nests colonially. After the breeding season, as many as 80,000 of these birds may occupy a single roost. While such aggregations are a spectacular sight, they create the possibility of disaster in hurricane season when violent storms occur near roosts.

Identification  23–27". A large white bird with black wingtips and a long, down-curved bill. The bill, face, and legs are red. Young birds are largely brown or mottled brown above.

Voice  Soft grunts and growls; a loud flight call: *urnk urnk.*

Habitat  Coastal marshes, mud flats, and swamps.

Range  Along the southeastern coast from Texas to Florida and north to southern North Carolina.

### White-faced Ibis *Plegadis chihi*

Two species of dark ibises occur in North America: the White-faced Ibis and the Glossy Ibis. Throughout much of the year these two species look virtually identical; during the nesting season, however, there are physical differences. Another useful aid to identification is geographical location. The White-faced Ibis is found primarily from Texas westward; the Glossy Ibis, from Louisiana eastward.

Identification    22–25". A large, overall dark bird with a long, down-curved bill and reddish eyes, bill, and legs. Breeding birds are largely chestnut-colored and, unlike breeding Glossy Ibises, have a narrow band of white feathers creating a border around the face.

Voice    Creaks, grunts, and croaks.

Habitat    Primarily freshwater marshes, but also brackish or salt marshes. Nests in reeds, grasses, or on floating mats of dead plants, several feet above the water.

Range    From North Dakota south to Texas and coastal Louisiana, and as far west as Oregon.

56

## Roseate Spoonbill *Ajaia ajaja*

The scientific name for the Roseate Spoonbill, pronounced "ah-EYE-ah ah-YA-ya," is the latinized version of a Brazilian Amerindian name. Such unusual nomenclature well suits a bird of such fantastical color and shape. Like most products of evolution, however, the spoonbill's strange physiognomy works well in the bird's habitat. The flattened, spatulate-shaped bill is used to feel for and capture crustaceans and fish as the bird wades in relatively shallow water. At one point, early in the 20th century, feather hunters had so decimated this species that less than three dozen Roseate Spoonbills survived. Populations have responded well to subsequent conservation efforts.

| | |
|---|---|
| Identification | 30–32". A large, mainly pink bird with a greenish head and broadly flattened bill. |
| Voice | A low croak or cluck. |
| Habitat | Shallow, coastal waters lined with mangroves, willows, or low bushes. |
| Range | Southern Florida and along the Texas coast; rare in Louisiana. |

## Wood Stork *Mycteria americana*

Only three members of the stork family occur in the New World, and only one of these may be found in North America. The Wood Stork is our only true stork. While not uncommon along the southeastern coast, this bird is on the United States Endangered Species list. In order to breed successfully, the Wood Stork requires an adequate and readily available supply of fish to feed its young. If water levels are too high to permit efficient foraging, Wood Storks will not nest.

Identification  40–44". A large, long-legged white bird with black tail and flight feathers. It is also known as a "flint head" for its gray-black featherless head. The heavy, dark, down-curved bill is yellowish in immature birds. In flight, the stork extends its legs and neck.

Voice  Normally silent except at nest, where young are quite noisy.

Habitat  Cypress swamps and mangroves; coastal shallows, ponds, and marshes on or near the coast.

Range  From the South Carolina coast throughout Florida and along the Gulf Coast to Texas.

### Mute Swan *Cygnus olor*

North America has two native swans—the Tundra Swan and the Trumpeter Swan—but the Mute Swan is an introduced species. Mute Swans were brought to the United States from Europe more than a century ago. Because they require, and are able to defend, large nesting territories, these swans often prevent native waterfowl from nesting in their traditional locales. The Mute Swan's aggressive behavior during the nesting season is not to be taken lightly; these massive birds have been known to attack and injure unsuspecting humans.

Identification 58–60". A very large, white bird with a wingspan to 8', an orange bill, and a black knob below the forehead. When a Mute Swan is at rest, it shows a downward tilt to the head and an S-shaped neck.

Voice Normally silent; occasionally hisses and grunts. Also rarely utters a loud trumpeting call.

Habitat Ponds, coastal lagoons, and open marshes.

Range From New England south to New Jersey, and around the Great Lakes.

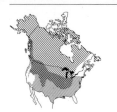

## Canada Goose *Branta canadensis*

The Canada Goose is a common sight throughout much of the United States. On migration, V-shaped strings of these geese often call attention to themselves with their clamorous honking. Canada Geese are also seen roosting on ponds and lakes or grazing in fields. Seemingly comfortable around humankind, this goose species regularly frequents golf courses, public parks, and neighborhood ponds. Because of their size and relative tameness, these geese are ideal subjects for making observations on bird behavior, especially during the nesting cycle.

| | |
|---|---|
| Identification | 22–45". A large waterfowl with a distinctive black neck and head and a white chin strap. Its body feathers are dusky below and dark brown above. |
| Voice | A loud, two-noted honk, with the second note higher in pitch than the first. |
| Habitat | Ponds, lakes, and other open waters; also feeds in fields, on golf courses, and in grasslands. |
| Range | Widespread in North America. |

## Wood Duck *Aix sponsa*

The male Wood Duck in full breeding plumage is an extraordinary sight. The patterning and colors on his head alone, a combination of glossy greens and bright reds, are as spectacular as those on any waterfowl in the world. While the female is definitely less decorative, her subtle hues of brown and blue are also a visual delight. As its name implies, this duck frequents forested areas, and its natural nesting sites include cavities in mature or dead trees.

| | |
|---|---|
| Identification | 17–20". Males have glossy green head feathers complete with a manelike crest. The eyes and base of the bill are bright red. Females are largely mouse-brown; however, there is a distinctive, tear-shaped, white eye-ring and a blue speculum. |
| Voice | In flight, a high pitched *wooo-eeek*. Also soft mews and peeps. The female's whining flight call is frequently heard. |
| Habitat | Wooded swamps, rivers, and ponds. In fall, freshwater marshes. |
| Range | From North Dakota east to Nova Scotia and south to Texas. Also the Pacific Northwest east to Montana, and California. |

66

### Green-winged Teal  *Anas crecca*

Of the three common teals of North America (the others are the Blue-winged Teal and the Cinnamon Teal), this is the smallest. On the wing, the Green-winged Teal is a delight to watch. Its rapid flight is regularly punctuated by sharp turns and twists. Although most Green-winged Teals winter in the southern United States and Mexico, they are an especially hardy species. Individuals regularly linger in the northerly parts of their range into early winter. In spring, Green-winged Teals are among the earliest migrants.

Identification 12–16". A small, dark duck. Males are overall grayish brown with a distinctive, chestnut-colored head and a contrasting swath of green from the eye to the nape. Females are largely buff-colored. In flight, the green speculum can be seen.

Voice Males emit short, high-pitched whistles; females quack.

Habitat Marshy ponds, lakes, and rivers.

Range Breeds primarily from Alaska throughout Canada and in the western U.S. Winters throughout the southern half of the U.S.

## American Black Duck *Anas rubripes*

American Black Ducks are **declining in numbers,** and the species is being pressured from several different directions. A reduction in the size of their wetland nesting habitat is a primary threat. The health of individual ducks is indirectly affected by the use of lead shot and pesticides, both of which introduce toxic substances into feeding areas. The American Black Duck as a species is also threatened by another duck—the Mallard. Because the two species readily interbreed, hybrids are becoming more common, and the number of "pure" American Black Ducks is declining.

Identification 19–22". Overall dark brown with a paler face and neck. The male's bill is yellow; the female's, greenish yellow. There is a purple speculum. In flight, seen from below, this duck appears dark, or blackish, with silvery wing linings.

Voice The quintessential duck quack.

Habitat Fresh- and saltwater marshes, ponds, swamps, and lakes.

Range An eastern bird. Breeds from Saskatchewan east to Prince Edward Island, south to New York. Winters south of its breeding range to South Carolina.

## Mallard *Anas platyrhynchos*

Ducks can be divided into two basic groups, the dabblers and the divers. Dabblers feed from the surface, using tilting motions that allow them to reach aquatic vegetation, seeds, and other food just below the surface. The Mallard is our most abundant dabbler. The progenitor of many duck species, the Mallard is capable of hybridizing with a wide variety of waterfowl, at times to the detriment of the other species (see American Black Duck, page 70). At home almost anywhere, the Mallard takes readily to public places.

Identification  18–27". The male's green head and yellow bill are distinctive. Males also have a chestnut-colored breast and a blue speculum bordered in white. Female Mallards are overall light brown and also have a blue speculum bordered in white.

Voice  Females utter a loud, descending series of quacks; males utter softer notes.

Habitat  Commonly found on any shallow body of fresh water.

Range  Widespread in North America.

### Northern Pintail *Anas acuta*

The Northern Pintail is one of the more abundant and widespread waterfowl species in North America. In winter, when inland ponds and marshes freeze over, these ducks head for the coast. There their diet of aquatic plants is supplemented by small fish, clams, and snails.

Identification 25–30". This duck's slender look is emphasized by its long neck and extended tail feathers. The drake's white neck and brown head are distinctive, with a sliver of white extending up to the side of the head. Females are overall pale buff.

Voice In courtship, males utter a two-noted whistle; females emit hoarse, descending quacks.

Habitat Prairie and tundra marshes and ponds on breeding grounds; in winter, inland ponds, marshes, and also coastal estuaries and salt marshes.

Range Breeds primarily in the North, from Alaska east to Prince Edward Island, and also in the western U.S. as far south as New Mexico. Winters on the West Coast south to Texas and along the East Coast and the Great Lakes.

74

## Blue-winged Teal *Anas discors*

On the prairies of the United States and Canada there are small ponds called "potholes" that serve as critical wetland resources, providing nesting habitats for many bird species. Many waterfowl, including this species, rely on these potholes as a place to raise young. Unfortunately, the Blue-winged Teal has suffered as prairie potholes have been drained to provide more land for farming. Less hardy than the Green-winged Teal (see page 68), this species normally winters south of the United States.

Identification  14–16". A small, fast-flying duck. There is a white crescent on the drake's gray-blue head. In flight, both males and females show the characteristic powder-blue wing patch.

Voice  Females utter a weak quack; males, a soft peeping or lisping.

Habitat  Freshwater ponds, marshes, creeks, and shallow lakes.

Range  Breeds from southeastern Alaska to the East Coast, and as far south as Texas. Winters from North Carolina south to Florida and along the Gulf Coast to Texas; also along the California coast.

## Cinnamon Teal *Anas cyanoptera*

The Cinnamon Teal is a western species, seldom encountered east of the Rocky Mountains. A majority of these birds spend the winter south of the United States. During March and early April they fly north to their breeding grounds. Unlike other ducks, which are often found in flocks, Cinnamon Teal are somewhat solitary and normally occur in pairs. Female Cinnamon Teal attend to the chick-rearing chores and may hatch up to a dozen ducklings per season. Normally, however, as is the case with most ducks, chick mortality to predators is high. Only a few of the young ducks will survive their first two months of life.

Identification 14–17". Drakes are characteristically rufous below and on the neck and head. Both sexes display a blue wing patch. Females are brown and rather plainly marked.

Voice Males utter a low chatter; females, a soft quacking.

Habitat Shallow lakes, ponds, prairie marshes, and sluggish streams bordered by grasses and reeds.

Range A western bird; breeds from Washington south to Texas; year-round in southwestern states.

## Hooded Merganser *Lophodytes cucullatus*

Mergansers are typical diving ducks, characteristically feeding below the surface of the water. While the Hooded Merganser is an excellent underwater swimmer and takes its share of fish, it also feeds on crustaceans and insects. In late winter and early spring, it is often possible to observe their interesting courtship displays. The drake customarily shows off his handsome crest and then arches his neck quickly backward so that his head nearly touches his back.

Identification  16–19". The drake is buff below with a white chest and black back and head. The contrasting white head patch and crested appearance are diagnostic. Females are light brown with a pale crest.

Voice  Hoarse grunts and croaks.

Habitat  Woodland ponds, lakes, and rivers, and sometimes saltwater creeks in winter.

Range  Breeds from southeasternmost Alaska south to Oregon, and from Manitoba east to Nova Scotia and south to Arkansas. Winters on the California coast, and from Mississippi to Florida and as far north as New England.

80

## Common Merganser  *Mergus merganser*

The Common Merganser is an underwater hunter whose diet consists mainly of fish. Once below the surface, this duck uses its expert swimming abilities to chase down minnow-sized fish. The merganser's bill is equipped with a toothlike edge that helps the bird hold onto its prey. This is the largest of the three North American merganser species (the others are the Hooded and the Red-breasted mergansers) and the largest wild duck likely to be seen at inland locations.

Identification  22–27". A large duck. The drake is recognized by his white breast, green head complete with crest feathers, and thin red bill. The female has a reddish-brown head and crest and a contrasting white throat area.

Voice  Harsh, rasping croaks.

Habitat  Usually inland, freshwater ponds and wooded rivers; in winter, occasionally found on salt bays.

Range  Widespread from eastern Alaska throughout Canada and the U.S. Winters throughout most of the U.S.

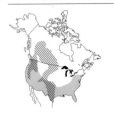

## Ruddy Duck *Oxyura jamaicensis*

Something of an oddball among North American waterfowl, the Ruddy Duck belongs to a small group called "stiff-tailed" ducks. In breeding plumage, the chunky drake, with its cocked tail, appears to be something of a caricature. Ruddy Ducks spend most of their time on the water and tend not to associate with other waterfowl. Expert divers, they gather food on the bottoms of ponds and lakes.

| | |
|---|---|
| **Identification** | 14–16". A small, chunky duck. Drakes in breeding plumage have a broad, pale blue bill and white cheek; the body feathers are rust-colored. Females are overall light brown, with the distinctive bill and body shape. |
| **Voice** | Usually silent except in courtship, when males utter continuous clucking and *chuck* notes. |
| **Habitat** | Freshwater marshes, lakes, and ponds with dense vegetation; in winter, on large bodies of water and occasionally on salt marshes. |
| **Range** | Breeds from British Columbia to Manitoba, south to New Mexico, and in the Northeast. Winters around the coastal perimeter of the U.S. and as far inland as Missouri. |

84

### Osprey *Pandion haliaetus*

North American Osprey populations were devastated by the use of DDT during the 1950s and 1960s. Toxic elements in DDT were passed up the food chain to fish, the Osprey's sole food source, and thence to the birds themselves. By the mid-1970s DDT had been largely banned, and Ospreys began to make a comeback, encouraged by man-made nesting platforms. The "fish hawk" is once again a fairly common coastal sight.

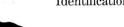

Identification  21–24". A large brown (the brown often appears black) and white bird regularly seen hovering and fishing along the coast or at larger lakes and rivers. Seen from below, it shows long, crooked wings with dark "wrist" patches. There is a dark, masklike line on the side of its face.

Voice  A loud, repeated whistle.

Habitat  Wetland habitats, especially coastal marshes, as well as lakes and rivers.

Range  Breeds from Alaska and Newfoundland south along both coasts; occasionally inland near lakes and rivers. Winters from southern California and the Gulf states south.

## American Swallow-tailed Kite *Elanoides forficatus*

This spectacular raptor flies with particular agility and
grace. Sociable by nature, it is often seen hunting in small
groups, swooping and gliding in and out of open woodland,
in seemingly effortless maneuvers. Perhaps its ability as an
aerialist accounts for the fact that it spends much of its time
in the air, seldom going to perch. The American Swallow-
tailed Kite even feeds in the air, taking a variety of insects,
lizards, and snakes. When thirsty it also stays on the wing,
drinking as it skims the surface of a pond or stream.

Identification 22–24". A black and white bird with pointed wings and a
deeply forked, swallowlike tail.

Voice A shrill, whistled *klee klee klee.*

Habitat Open southern woodlands and adjacent wetlands, including
river bottoms.

Range Texas, east along the Gulf Coast through Florida, and north
to South Carolina. Winters south of the U.S.

### Snail Kite  *Rostrhamus sociabilis*

The Snail Kite is one of numerous species in southern Florida that have suffered because of the ever-growing needs of humans. It feeds almost exclusively on apple snails whose populations are being drastically reduced as wetlands are drained for development. Fewer than two dozen birds survived in Florida in the mid-1960s. Last-minute conservation efforts seem to have been effective, however, as counts of more than 700 birds were made in the 1980s.

Identification    16–18". A handsome raptor; adult males are overall slate-black with bright red legs. Adult females and immatures are brown above and darkly streaked below, with a white throat and forehead patch. In flight, birds show a characteristic tail pattern: a broad white area at the base, a wide black band in the middle, and a narrow buff terminal band.

Voice    A repetitious cackle when disturbed, as well as a harsh greeting call.

Habitat    Freshwater wetlands.

Range    In the U.S., restricted to southern Florida, but also found in the American tropics.

### Bald Eagle  *Haliaeetus leucocephalus*

The Bald Eagle has turned out to be more of a symbol than our forefathers might have expected. Less than two centuries after it was chosen as our national emblem, it was listed as threatened or endangered in all states except Alaska. By the 1970s its populations had plummeted, and the eagle was fast becoming symbolic of widespread habitat loss and pesticide poisoning. Fortunately, recovery programs have helped, and Bald Eagles are once again nesting successfully over much of their former range.

| | |
|---|---|
| Identification | 31–32". The adult Bald Eagle is nearly unmistakable, given its large size, dark body, and snow-white head and tail. Young birds are brown overall and variously streaked with white. |
| Voice | Harsh, metallic cackles. |
| Habitat | Almost invariably adjacent to wetlands, especially along coastlines and around large lakes and rivers. |
| Range | Widespread in Alaska; more restricted in the contiguous 48 states, but found regularly along the Pacific and Atlantic coasts, in the Northwest, and in Florida. |

### Northern Harrier *Circus cyaneus*

Formerly called the Marsh Hawk, this species is the only North American representative of the harrier group. These birds are noted for their unusual hunting behavior. They fly only a few feet off the ground over open country and marshes, ever ready to pounce on small rodents, various reptiles, and occasionally even birds. A dish-shaped face enables the hawk to locate its prey through sound, a unique attribute among North America's diurnal raptors.

Identification  16–24". A slim, long-winged, long-tailed raptor whose most obvious field mark is a conspicuous white rump. The back-and-forth, low-to-the-ground, slightly rocking flight is also a good clue to identification.

Voice  Normally silent; at times utters a shrill *kee kee kee* from the nest.

Habitat  Coastal and inland marshes, as well as open meadows, fields, and grasslands.

Range  Breeds from Alaska east to the eastern seaboard, south through the central U.S. Winters across most of the southern U.S.

## King Rail *Rallus elegans*

In general, rails are secretive marsh birds that are more frequently heard than seen. Knowing the various rail vocalizations is important in identification. The King Rail occurs in freshwater situations, as well as in brackish areas. It is one of two species of large rails in North America. The other, the Clapper Rail (*R. longirostris*), is most often associated with saltwater marshes. Some biologists feel these look-alikes are actually one species.

Identification 15–19". A relatively large (compare the Virginia Rail, page 98), long-billed, chickenlike bird. Largely rust-colored below and on the neck and face. There is black-and-white barring on the flanks. The back is dark brown and streaked.

Voice A series of ticking sounds, such as would be made by tapping two large stones together; also a rapid, repeated grunting, like the sound of a plunger clearing a drain.

Habitat Freshwater swamps and marshes.

Range Widespread across the eastern half of the U.S., from Minnesota to Massachusetts and south to Texas and Florida.

## Virginia Rail  *Rallus limicola*

The Virginia Rail is well adapted for life in the marsh. Its coloration blends well with the mud and wetland plants. Its relatively narrow body allows it to wind its way easily through a tangle of plants. Biologists describe this body shape as "compressed laterally"; it is, in layman's terms, "thin as a rail." The bird's large feet allow it to walk in muddy areas and even on floating vegetation. The long bill probes in the mud for insects and worms.

Identification
9–11". A relatively small bird (compare the King Rail, page 96) with a reddish bill and rust-colored underparts. Its face is grayish, and the flanks show some barring. The back and sides are brown to reddish.

Voice
A series of clicking sounds: *kidick-kidick-kidick-kidick*; also a rapid series of descending grunts.

Habitat
Freshwater and brackish marshes; also salt marshes in winter.

Range
Breeds from British Columbia east to Nova Scotia and as far south as Texas. Winters commonly along the East and West coasts.

98

### Sora *Porzana carolina*

Fairly common in extensive wetlands, Soras frequently can be located by their calls. They are best sighted at dusk or dawn, feeding along the muddy edges of inland marshes. The Sora's nest is constructed of cattails and other reeds and grasses and affixed to the emergent vegetation just above the waterline. Spring rains sometimes flood the nest, which is then abandoned.

| | |
|---|---|
| **Identification** | 8–10". A relatively small rail with a short, stubby, yellowish bill. There are black feathers on the face and throat of breeding adults, as well as barring below. |
| **Voice** | A slurred *ker-wee, ker-wee,* with rising inflection; a sharp *keek!*; also a descending series of piped notes. |
| **Habitat** | Primarily freshwater and brackish marshes, as well as rice and grain fields. |
| **Range** | Breeds from British Columbia to California and east to Pennsylvania. Winters from Lower California to the Carolinas. |

## Purple Gallinule  *Porphyrula martinica*

Gallinules, chickenlike members of the rail family (Rallidae), are closely related to cranes. The adult Purple Gallinule's spectacular plumage makes it one of the more attractive water birds. While its normal range in the United States is restricted to the Southeast, the Purple Gallinule has a reputation for showing up in unexpected places—sometimes as far north as southern Canada. Such seasonal wandering or vagrancy is known to occur in many of North America's birds, and it adds spice to the pastime of birdwatching. While surprises are possible at any time, most vagrancy tends to be noted in the fall.

Identification   11–13". A chicken-sized marsh bird with large feet. It is blue below and green above; its red bill has a yellow tip. Juvenile birds show some green and blue coloring but are largely pale brown.

Voice   Henlike cackling, squawks, and grunts.

Habitat   Freshwater swamps and marshes with pickerelweed.

Range   Breeds in the southeastern U.S. and the Gulf Coast inland to Texas. Winters in Florida, and along the Gulf Coast.

102

## Common Moorhen *Gallinula chloropus*

Formerly called the Common Gallinule, this species is actually uncommon but fairly widespread in eastern North America. The legs and feet of gallinules are especially well adapted for life in the marsh. Common Moorhens can actually climb through dense, reedy vegetation by grasping first one stalk and then another. Their long toes distribute their weight, allowing them to walk over muddy ground as well as across lily pads and other broad-leaved water plants.

| | |
|---|---|
| Identification | 13". A chicken-sized marsh bird that is mainly gray-black with a red shield on its forehead and a yellow-tipped red bill. It has a white rump and a narrow white line on the flanks. |
| Voice | A wide variety of harsh squawks, henlike clucks, and screams. |
| Habitat | Freshwater marshes, ponds, and the edges of rivers with cattails, willows, and other vegetation. |
| Range | From California south to New Mexico, and from Oklahoma east to southern New England and south to the Gulf Coast. |

### American Coot *Fulica americana*

Technically a member of the rail family, the American Coot behaves more like a waterfowl. While its close relatives the gallinules and rails tend to stay in heavy cover or along water edges, the coot regularly swims in open water. There it combines the strategies of both diving and dabbling ducks to feed on a variety of aquatic plants and arthropods. While the coot's strange-sounding vocalization may be the source of the phrase "crazy as a coot," it might refer as well to his unorthodox behavior while becoming airborne. The American Coot patters along on the water, flailing its wings in a comical and seemingly labored takeoff.

Identification 15". A chunky, slate-gray, chickenlike bird with a white bill and white undertail feathers. It often bobs its head as it swims. In flight, its wing shows a white trailing edge.

Voice A variety of clucks, cackles, and grunts.

Habitat Freshwater ponds, lakes, and open marshes; winters on both fresh and salt water.

Range Widespread in southern Canada and throughout the U.S. Winters mainly in the southern U.S.

**Limpkin** *Aramus guarauna*

The Limpkin is unique. Although it looks like a heron and acts like a rail, this species is actually the only surviving member of a largely prehistoric family of wading birds. The Limpkin itself had a recent brush with extinction. Because the flesh is tasty, Limpkins were nearly hunted out in the early part of the 20th century. Fortunately, conservation efforts and protective legislation turned the tide, and Limpkin populations have recovered. Two folk names for this bird give insight into its behavior. The nickname "crying bird" refers to its distinctive wail; it is also called "crippled bird," in reference to its halting gait.

Identification  25–28". A heronlike bird with long legs and a long, slightly down-curved bill. It is overall gray-brown but has heavy white streaking and spotting, especially on the head, neck, and back.

Voice  A loud, wailing cry: *krrreeo!*

Habitat  Freshwater marshes and swamps with open water channels and vegetation.

Range  Southern Georgia and Florida. Nonmigratory.

108

## Sandhill Crane *Grus canadensis*

Cranes are magnificent, long-legged birds well known
for their courtship rituals, which involve complex dances.
Fifteen species of cranes occur worldwide. It is still possible
to see spectacular numbers of Sandhill Cranes on migration,
at such staging areas as the Platte River in Nebraska, but
draining of wetlands has endangered much of the population.

Identification 34–48". A large bird, overall gray with a distinctive red
cap. Body feathers are often stained brown by mineral
deposits in the water. In flight, the head, neck, and legs
are outstretched. In general, cranes may be distinguished
from herons and egrets by the long feathers that drape over
their rumps.

Voice Loud, trumpeting calls: *karrroooah.*

Habitat Marshy tundra, prairie ponds, and damp meadows,
marshes, and grasslands; dry fields in winter.

Range Resident in Florida and parts of the Gulf Coast; migratory
populations breed in Alaska and the Far North into
northern Canada, the Great Lakes region, and parts of the
northwestern states.

## Whooping Crane *Grus americana*

During the 20th century the Whooping Crane has come close to extinction several times. In the mid-1940s less than two dozen Whooping Cranes survived in the wild. Preservation efforts have increased numbers to approximately 200 birds, and experimental programs to introduce Whooping Cranes into new areas are under way. The best place to see these stately birds is at their wintering quarters in Aransas National Wildlife Refuge in Texas.

Identification 52". A large bird. Adult birds are overall white with red areas on the face. Young birds have tan heads and necks; their bodies are white with brown mottling. In flight, adults show black primaries and their heads, necks, and legs are outstretched.

Voice A loud, trumpeting *kerloo! ker-lee-oo!*

Habitat Prairie marshes.

Range Breeds in Wood Buffalo National Park, Alberta, Canada. Winters in Aransas National Wildlife Refuge on the Gulf Coast of Texas.

### Killdeer *Charadrius vociferus*

One of our more common and widespread shorebirds, the Killdeer is distinguished by the fact that it regularly nests at inland areas. In fact, this species has a reputation for nesting almost anywhere. A simple scrape on the ground of a field, airport, or even a vacant lot is common. The Killdeer will also nest on flat-top roofs or at construction sites. Nesting Killdeer seem ever ready to present their famous "broken wing" display, intended to draw a predator away from the nest.

Identification   9–11". A robin-sized shorebird, brown above and white below. It shows two black breast bands and, in flight or display, a rust-colored rump.

Voice   A high-pitched *kee-dee! kee-dee!* or *dee dee dee!* often heard in flight.

Habitat   Plowed fields and open areas such as golf courses and meadows; also shores.

Range   Widespread from southeastern Alaska throughout Canada and the U.S.

114

### Lesser Yellowlegs *Tringa flavipes*

This bird and its close relative the Greater Yellowlegs (*T. melanoleuca*) are included in a group of shorebirds often referred to as "tattlers." Hunters used this term for shorebirds that sound an alarm by vocalizing loudly when approached too closely. The alarm alerts all the birds in the area, and it is usually followed by a swift exit of the entire flock. While the Lesser Yellowlegs lives up to its nickname, especially on its Arctic breeding grounds, it is also known to be tame at times. On migration it is not unusual to see small flocks of Lesser Yellowlegs traveling together.

Identification | 10½". A delicate-looking shorebird with long yellow legs. It has salt-and-pepper feathers above and white below; the overall appearance is quite dark at times. The Lesser has a shorter and thinner bill than the Greater Yellowlegs.

Voice | A soft, two-noted whistle: *tu-tu! tu-tu!*

Habitat | Mud flats, grassy marshes, and shores of ponds, lakes, and rivers.

Range | Breeds from Alaska east to Ontario. Winters along the southern Atlantic and Gulf coasts, and southern California.

116

### Solitary Sandpiper  *Tringa solitaria*

Whereas many shorebirds seek the safety of the flock, the Solitary Sandpiper seems disposed to stay by itself, at least on migration. A visitor to this species' breeding grounds might be surprised to find it and other shorebirds perched in trees. In fact, the Solitary Sandpiper often makes use of another bird's abandoned nest, well up in a tree. This behavior is an example of some birds' tendency to behave in very different ways on their wintering grounds, on migration, and on their nesting territories.

Identification    8½". A medium-sized shorebird, overall dark gray above and light below with a conspicuous eye-ring and greenish-gray legs. The neck and upper breast are streaked with brown. In flight, birds show a tail that is barred black and white.

Voice    Usually three-syllabled: *peet-weet-weet.*

Habitat    Freshwater streams, swamps, ponds, and bogs.

Range    Breeds from Alaska east to Labrador. Winters mainly south of the U.S.

### Spotted Sandpiper *Actitis macularia*

Whereas most shorebirds seen in North America are migrants, on their way to and from more northerly breeding grounds, the Spotted Sandpiper is one of the few species that nest throughout most of the contiguous 48 states. The nests are simple, grass-lined scrapes, usually well hidden in the vegetation surrounding various types of wetlands. During the winter months some Spotted Sandpipers can be found along the Gulf Coast, but a majority go farther south to Central and South America.

Identification  7½". A medium-sized sandpiper most easily recognized by its teetering or bobbing gait. In breeding plumage, the bird is boldly spotted below and brown above, with heavy barring. In flight, it shows a white line running lengthwise down the wing.

Voice  A clear, whistled *peet-weet*; also *weet, weet, weet*.

Habitat  Common along any shoreline, along coastal or inland waters.

Range  Breeds throughout most of North America, except the southernmost U.S., where it winters.

## Least Sandpiper *Calidris minutilla*

Identifying sandpipers presents many challenges. Expert observers rely on habitat and time of year as well as a variety of physical characteristics. This species and the Pectoral Sandpiper (see page 124) are often mistaken for one another. They look similar, and both occur in grassy areas along wet edges or in meadows. The key to separating the two species is size: The Pectoral Sandpiper is about three inches larger than the Least Sandpiper. Least Sandpipers nest at the edge of the boreal forest and the treeless arctic tundra. Their grass-lined nests typically hold four eggs, incubated by the male.

Identification 6". A small bird, brown above, white below, and often with biblike markings on the breast. The yellowish-green legs are not always obvious in poor light.

Voice A clear *treep, treep, treep;* also a whinny.

Habitat Mud flats along coasts, marshes, wet fields, and beaches of salt or fresh waters.

Range Breeds in Alaska and northern Canada. Winters from the southern U.S. south.

## Pectoral Sandpiper *Calidris melanotos*

Like many of the shorebirds seen in North America, the Pectoral Sandpiper is a long-distance migrant. It travels thousands of miles annually, from South American wintering areas to high Arctic breeding grounds. The Arctic summer is short-lived, but the sun never sets, and swarms of insects are readily available for feeding ravenous chicks. If all goes well a new generation of birds is reared. After a few busy weeks, with the onset of the Arctic winter, the Pectoral Sandpipers must abandon their breeding grounds and make the long journey south to more habitable winter quarters.

| | |
|---|---|
| Identification | 9". A medium-sized shorebird with characteristic biblike markings on the breast and yellowish legs. Basically brown above and light below. (See Least Sandpiper, page 122.) |
| Voice | On breeding grounds, males inflate neck and breast to produce low, booming sounds. Alarm calls include a sharp *brrrp* or *krick, krick.* |
| Habitat | Wet meadows, golf courses, and grassy pools. |
| Range | Breeds on the Arctic coasts and Hudson Bay. Winters in South America. |

## Common Snipe *Gallinago gallinago*

During the latter half of the 19th century, many of our shorebird populations were decimated by hunters. No limit were in effect, and tens of thousands of birds were shot eac year, including thousands of Common Snipes. The Common Snipe is still considered a game bird, although limits are now strictly regulated.

Identification  10½–11½". A medium-sized shorebird, regularly found inland. It is brown above and white below, with a long bill, striped crown, and rusty tail.

Voice  A sharp *scaip!* in alarm or in flight; at nest site, a repeated, whistled *wheet, wheet, wheet* or *whuck, whuck, whuck;* in territorial display flight, the tail feathers produce an eerie, whistling sound as air passes through them.

Habitat  Prefers wet meadows and fields, freshwater marshes, bogs, and ponds; also salt marshes during migration.

Range  Breeds from Alaska to Newfoundland, south to California and Pennsylvania. Winters in the southern U.S. and northward along both coasts.

## American Woodcock  *Scolopax minor*

Observing the male American Woodcock's courtship display is well worth the effort involved in tracking down a breeding pair. At dusk at an active territory, the first clue to the woodcocks' presence may be the male's nasal call. It is typically repeated several times before the bird takes to the air. His spiraling descent is characterized by a series of wing whistles and chirps. The male is almost certain to repeat this display numerous times to impress potential mates.

Identification 11". A chunky, medium-sized shorebird that regularly nests at inland locales. It is brown above and buff below, with black lateral bars on the crown and a long bill.

Voice During breeding season, the male emits a nasal *peent*, repeated about every two seconds, from the ground before flying upward. Descending from his territorial flight display, he utters a series of twittering chirps.

Habitat Moist, damp woods near open fields and clearings.

Range Widespread across the eastern half of the U.S. and southeastern Canada.

128

## Wilson's Phalarope  *Phalaropus tricolor*

Wilson's is one of three species of phalaropes that occur in North America; the others are the Red-necked Phalarope (*P. lobatus*) and the Red Phalarope (*P. fulicarius*). The latter two species spend much of their lives at sea. Wilson's Phalarope, however, may be found inland on migration, and it regularly breeds at inland wetlands, especially in the West. Like other phalaropes, the female and male Wilson's seem to have switched gender roles. It is the female that has brighter plumage and leads the courtship ritual. The male often builds the nest and takes responsibility for incubating.

Identification  9". A medium-sized shorebird that is gray and rusty above, pale below. It has a long, thin bill and a black eye-patch that extends back along the neck. This bird sometimes spins around on the surface of a pond or lake while feeding.

Voice  Soft croaks and quacks.

Habitat  Prairie marshes, shallow ponds, and marshy pools.

Range  Breeds from British Columbia and southwestern Canada south to Nevada and the central U.S. Winters in southern South America.

### Franklin's Gull  *Larus pipixcan*

More than two dozen species of gulls occur in North America. As most are found in coastal habitats, the common term "seagull" is appropriate. But it does not apply to Franklin's Gull. On its breeding grounds, this species is strictly an inland resident. In its summer home on the western plains, Franklin's Gull is often referred to as the "prairie dove." Flocks are typically seen in agricultural areas or actually following farm machinery in search of insects.

Identification — 13½–15½". A relatively small gull recognized by its black hood and white underparts. The upper surface of the wings is gray. The pattern of the wingtip is distinctive, characterized by an area of white separating the gray-colored feathers from the black outer primaries, which are tipped with white. Legs, feet, and bill are reddish.

Voice — A shrill *kuk-kuk-kuk,* and *weeh-ah, weeh-ah.*

Habitat — Prairie lakes, marshes, and small ponds.

Range — Breeds from Alberta to Manitoba and south from Oregon to Iowa. Winters off the west coast of South America.

### Ring-billed Gull *Larus delawarensis*

Gulls go through a series of plumage changes that present a challenge to birdwatchers. The Ring-billed, a so-called three-year gull, takes on a different look in each of its first three years. Although common on the coasts, it is regularly found inland and typically nests near freshwater habitats. Ring-billed Gull populations seem to be increasing, and these gulls are often found at dumps and around fast-food restaurants, where food scraps are plentiful.

Identification 18–21". The adult has a white head and underparts with a gray back and black-tipped gray wings. The legs and eyes are yellowish, and the yellow bill has a black ring near its tip. Young birds are overall gray and brown with dark bills and grayish legs.

Voice A high, shrill *ky-eow.*

Habitat Islands or shores of inland lakes; wet, plowed fields; garbage dumps; in winter, also along coastal shores.

Range Widely dispersed throughout prairies of Canada and the U.S., Washington and Oregon, and the Great Lakes region. Winters along U.S. coasts as far inland as Kansas.

134

## California Gull  *Larus californicus*

Like the other species of gulls covered in this volume, the California Gull is regularly found inland during the breeding season. And, like Franklin's and Ring-billed gulls, these birds rely on insects as an important part of their diet. In fact, the California Gull is celebrated as something of a protector in the Mormon tradition because these were the birds that eliminated large numbers of locusts threatening the early settlers' crops.

Identification 20–23". A large gull. Overall white with a gray mantle and wings; there is a black outer portion of the wings, marked white at their tips. This gull has dark eyes, black and red spots near the tip of its yellow bill, and yellowish-green legs.

Voice A repeated *kee-yah*.

Habitat A western bird of inland lakes and marshes; winters along the coast.

Range Alberta and Saskatchewan south to Wyoming and Utah and west to California. Winters along the West Coast; very rare along the East and Gulf coasts.

136

## Caspian Tern *Sterna caspia*

Terns are closely related to gulls but in general are somewhat sleeker, with relatively longer wings and forked tails. The Caspian Tern is the largest North American tern. It breeds at scattered colonies along the coast and inland. In and around such colonies the Caspian Tern's distinctive vocalization often calls attention to its presence. Like other terns, this species hovers over the water before diving to capture minnows and other small fish.

Identification   19–23". A grayish-white bird with a stout reddish-orange bill and black cap. Seen from below, extensive areas of the wingtips are dark. In winter the cap is gray. The forehead is also gray. In the similar Royal Tern, the forehead is white in winter-plumaged birds.

Voice   A loud, harsh *kar-rreeow* or *ga-ga-gaaah.*

Habitat   Inland lakes, rivers, and seacoasts.

Range   Widely dispersed and scattered throughout North America, except the Far North. Summer concentrations are found in the Canadian prairie provinces, California, and the Great Lakes. Winters along the Gulf Coast.

138

### Forster's Tern *Sterna forsteri*

Like other tern species, Forster's Tern is normally found around water. Although it obtains some of its food in typical ternlike fashion, by diving into the water to capture small fish, Forster's Tern is also adept at catching flying insects. These birds are regularly observed sweeping low over marsh vegetation in search of dragonflies, damselflies, and other insect prey.

Identification   14–16¼". Similar to the Common Tern in having a black cap and nape, gray upperparts, white underparts, and reddish legs and bill. However, it has a deeply forked tail and a frosty look to the upper primaries. In winter plumage, the bill is black and the black head markings are reduced to an area forming an eye-patch.

Voice   A raspy *zraa* or *zrurr;* also a shrill *pip-pip* or *kit, kit, kit.*

Habitat   Inland and coastal marshes and seacoasts.

Range   Breeds from the Canadian prairie provinces south to Colorado and west to California; also on the mid-Atlantic coast. Winters along the southeastern and Gulf coasts and the southern California coast.

## Least Tern *Sterna antillarum*

Breeding populations of Least Terns, the smallest tern species in North America, are found on the coasts and inland. Least Terns are adversely affected by human intrusions into their nesting areas along beaches, as well as by water-control projects on inland waters. Consequently, this species is considered endangered over much of its North American breeding range. Like many bird species, the Least Tern will often abandon its nest if a disturbance, either natural or man-made, occurs in or near breeding colonies. Effective conservation measures, including signs and fences, protect colonies in some areas.

| | |
|---|---|
| Identification | 8½–9½". The smallest North American tern. Gray above and white below, with a black cap and a petite yellow bill. |
| Voice | A repeated, two-syllable *dee-dee;* also a sharp *kit, kit.* |
| Habitat | Beaches and sandbars along shallow rivers and lakes and along coasts. |
| Range | Breeds along the West and East coasts and along major inland rivers. Winters in the tropics. |

## Black Tern *Chlidonias niger*

In breeding plumage, this small, dainty tern is unlike any other North American tern. At rest, its black body and dark wings are distinctive. Black Terns nest at inland marshes and construct their floating nests from cattails, canes, and other available vegetation. At times this species will even take advantage of a muskrat house, using it as a platform or which to nest. In the breeding season, Black Terns are found mainly at inland locales; during their movements to and from South America, however, they may be observed along the coast.

Identification
9–10¼". The black bill, head, and body of a breeding adult are distinctive. On nonbreeding adults, below, the wing is dusky gray; above, the wing is dark slate-gray. Molting adults take on a calico appearance, and juvenile birds show a good deal of mottled brown on the back and head.

Voice
A sharp, shrill *kip-kip-kip;* also other shrill screams.

Habitat
Inland marshes and prairie sloughs.

Range
Breeds from southern Canada south to central California and east to northern New England. Winters in the tropics.

### Belted Kingfisher *Ceryle alcyon*

The Belted Kingfisher is a regular feature of ponds, lakes, and rivers throughout much of North America. A rattled flight call is often the first hint of this kingfisher's presence. With a little patient searching, the observer will soon discover one or more of its favored perches, from which it flies out to hover over the water and then dive for fish. The female of this species is unusual in that she is the more colorful of the sexes. Also somewhat unexpected is the Belted Kingfisher's nest site, which is at the end of an excavated tunnel, typically in a sandy bank.

Identification | 11–14½". A large-headed bird with a distinctive crest and a big bill. Generally slate-blue above and white below. There is a broad blue band across the upper breast; females have an additional rust-colored band on the belly.

Voice | In flight, a loud, prolonged rattle.

Habitat | Banks of lakes and rivers and other clear fishing waters.

Range | Widespread in North America.

### Green Kingfisher *Chloroceryle americana*

Of North America's three kingfishers, this is the smallest. The Green Kingfisher's restricted range, small size, and rather inconspicuous manner require birdwatchers to make special efforts. Southern Texas is the best place to look. Many birders have seen this bird at the Santa Anna Wildlife Refuge in the Rio Grande Valley; others have spotted it along the Rio Frio or at Lost Maples State Park in the Texas Hill Country. The Green Kingfisher tends not to hover while fishing but darts from its streamside perch into the water.

| | |
|---|---|
| Identification | 7–8½". A small bird, without the Belted Kingfisher's ragged crest. Basically green above and white below, with a large bill, and white outer tail feathers in flight. The male shows a rust-colored breast band; the female, a band of dark spots. |
| Voice | In flight, a *cheep* note; also a sharp twitter. At nest, a repeated *tick*. |
| Habitat | Shaded streams and rivers. |
| Range | Rio Grande Valley and Edwards Plateau in Texas; occasionally in southeastern Arizona. |

### Willow Flycatcher *Empidonax trailii*

Some bird species look so much alike that even experts can't tell them apart. Until fairly recently, the Willow Flycatcher and the Alder Flycatcher (*E. alnorum*) were considered one species. Several sharp-eared researchers, however, noticed that two distinct types of song are given by these birds. Ultimately, they were declared different species, as ornithologists uncovered other differences. The Willow and Alder flycatchers belong to a group called the Empidonax flycatchers, which is known for its difficult identifications.

| | |
|---|---|
| Identification | 6". A smallish, rather inconspicuous and drab flycatcher with faint white eye-rings, obvious wingbars, and a yellowish wash on the belly. Best identified by its song. |
| Voice | A buzzy or wheezy *fitz-bew*, or *pit-speer*. The song of the similar Alder Flycatcher is more like *peet-sa*. |
| Habitat | Swampy thickets, particularly with willows; also mountain meadows and old orchards. |
| Range | Breeds from southern British Columbia east to New England, and as far south as New Mexico. Winters south of the U.S. |

### Great Kiskadee  *Pitangus sulphuratus*

Although widespread in Latin America, the Great Kiskadee has a restricted range in North America—it is another of the Texas specialties. Fortunately, this handsome flycatcher is anything but shy and retiring, and so is relatively easy to locate in its range. The Great Kiskadee's flashy yellow underparts, highly vocal manner, and bulky, conspicuous nest all aid in tracking down and identifying it. Kiskadees often hunt from a highly visible perch, flying out, at times in a manner similar to that of kingfishers, to capture large insects and minnows.

| | |
|---|---|
| Identification | 10½". A large flycatcher, brown above and yellow below, with a black-and-white striped head and a relatively heavy bill. The bird's yellow crown patch is normally concealed. |
| Voice | A loud, piercing *kis-ka-dee*; noisy chatter. |
| Habitat | Streamside thickets and lakes; also orchards, parks, and about towns. |
| Range | Rio Grande Valley in Texas; rarely southeastern Arizona. |

### Tree Swallow *Tachycineta bicolor*

Although the Cliff Swallows of Capistrano are more famous, returning Tree Swallows signal the onset of spring in many areas of North America. Actually, many Tree Swallows overwinter in the extreme southern United States. Whereas this species' summer diet consists mainly of insects, winter flocks often feed on bayberry. Among the great spectacles of fall are the enormous flocks of migratory Tree Swallows on their way south. At times, a flock may consist of hundreds of thousands of swallows.

Identification 5–6¼". A small bird that is dark above and white below. In good light the greenish to bluish iridescent coloration on the upper surfaces is apparent. Young birds are muddy brown above and may show a faint breast band.

Voice A constant, liquid twitter and chatter.

Habitat Open wooded areas near marshes, ponds, or rivers.

Range Breeds over most of North America, except the Far North and the southernmost states. Winters from southern California east to Florida and as far north as Long Island, New York.

154

## Northern Rough-winged Swallow
*Stelgidopteryx serripennis*

Taken together, the common and scientific names of this species are almost as long as the bird itself. The descriptive phrase "rough-winged" refers to tiny recurved hooks on the primary wing feathers that feel rough to the touch. Ornithologists are uncertain as to the exact function of these hooks. Northern Rough-winged Swallows choose a wide variety of nesting sites, including nest holes within Bank Swallow colonies, natural cavities along streamsides, or even small burrows high on the sides of mountains.

Identification  5–5¾". A small bird, mainly dark above and light below, that may be confused with the juvenile Tree Swallow (see page 154). The characteristic brownish wash on the chin, throat, and upper breast is not found on Tree Swallows.

Voice  Normally silent, but may emit buzzy notes.

Habitat  Along steep riverbanks, in gravel pits, or in sand or clay pits.

Range  Widespread throughout the U.S., from southern British Columbia and along the border south.

156

## Fish Crow *Corvus ossifragus*

There are half a dozen species of large black birds in North America that fit the generalized description of the familiar American Crow, including four kinds of crows and two species of raven. The Fish Crow is slightly smaller than the American Crow but is virtually indistinguishable in the field from its close relative. The two are best distinguished by voice. The eastern and largely coastal-plain range of the Fish Crow may also be of aid in sorting out the two species.

**Identification**  17". A large, black bird, slightly smaller and glossier than the familiar American Crow but best distinguished by voice.

**Voice**  A nasal *eh-eh*, very different from the caw of the American Crow, and *kwok*. Young American Crows also utter *kwok* sounds during breeding season.

**Habitat**  Favors coastal country in the North; marshes, rivers, streams, and beaches in the South. May also be found inland along rivers and swamps.

**Range**  An eastern bird; from Massachusetts south to Florida and the Gulf Coast to southeastern Texas, and inland along major rivers.

158

### Marsh Wren *Cistothorus palustris*

Once known as the Long-billed Marsh Wren, this is one of several species of birds that are more often heard than seen. In fact, the song of these wrens was the initial clue that the so-called Marsh Wren is actually two species. Marsh Wrens in the East have a relatively limited song vocabulary, while those in the West are known for their numerous song variations. Researchers have also established that they do not interbreed. As a result, birdwatchers may soon have another species to add to their lists.

| | |
|---|---|
| Identification | 5". A small, sparrow-sized wren, dark above with a white throat and chest and a buff belly. There is a solid dark crown, a white eye-line, and a streaked back. |
| Voice | A loud rattle; also a complex series of bubbly or reedy notes. |
| Habitat | Freshwater or brackish marshes edged with reeds. |
| Range | Breeds from southern Canada to California and east to New England, and along the Atlantic and Gulf coasts. Winters in the southern U.S., from California south and east through Texas to Florida. |

### American Dipper *Cinclus mexicanus*

Certainly one of North America's more interesting species, and one of only four dippers in the world, the American Dipper at first seems part duck and part songbird. It feeds by actually walking along the bottom of fast-moving mountain streams in search of insect larvae. The dipper is an excellent swimmer and can even use its wings to "fly" through the water. An enlarged oil gland provides the necessary waterproofing for the feathers. Closely related to wrens and thrushes, the American Dipper often builds its nest under a bridge, close to its unusual feeding "grounds."

| | |
|---|---|
| Identification | 7–8½". Like a chunky, short-tailed robin in shape; overall sooty gray with a dark bill. Juvenile birds are light gray above and mottled below, with a pinkish bill. |
| Voice | A loud, ringing song of whistles and trills that can be heard over the sound of rushing water. |
| Habitat | Clear, rushing, mountain streams. |
| Range | A western bird; from Alaska south through the Rockies and the Pacific mountains. May move to lower elevations in winter. |

162

### Yellow Warbler *Dendroica petechia*

Some birdwatchers consider warblers the butterflies of the feathered world. Approximately four dozen species of wood warblers are summer residents of North America, and their diverse plumages and interesting songs are a challenge and delight to bird enthusiasts. The Yellow Warbler is one of the more common species. A potential threat to Yellow Warblers is cowbirds. These nest parasites regularly lay their eggs in the warblers' nests, often at the expense of their unknowing hosts, who then raise the cowbird chicks.

| | |
|---|---|
| Identification | 4½–5¼". A sparrow-sized bird; largely yellow with darker wing feathers. There is rusty streaking on the male's chest. |
| Voice | A clear, loud, whistled *sweet, sweet, sweet! sweeter than sweet!* Call note is a down-slurred *cheep*. |
| Habitat | Brushy thickets near water, edges of woodlands, and suburban parks. |
| Range | Widespread across most of North America, except the Far North and the Gulf states. |

### **Prothonotary Warbler** *Protonotaria citrea*

Unlike the Yellow Warbler (see page 164), which ranges widely across North America, the Prothonotary Warbler is restricted to the eastern United States. Southern swamplands are its usual summer abode, and its bright golden, almost fiery plumage stands in marked contrast to the shadowy, cypress-lined banks along which it lives. Whereas most warblers build their nests from plant parts, the Prothonotary Warbler lives in the natural cavities supplied by streamside trees. Its nest is often parasitized by Brown-headed Cowbirds.

| | |
|---|---|
| Identification | 5½". A bit larger than the average wood warbler, this species has a golden yellow head and underparts and slate-gray wings. The bill is noticeably larger than in most warblers. |
| Voice | A loud, clear *sweet-sweet-sweet-sweet-sweet-sweet*. |
| Habitat | Wooded marshes, swamps, and streams with dead trees. |
| Range | Wisconsin south to eastern Texas, and east to the Appalachians, and from southern New England to Florida. |

166

## Northern Waterthrush *Seiurus noveboracensis*

The Northern Waterthrush is actually a warbler. Like its close relative the Louisiana Waterthrush (see page 170), it does resemble the North American spot-breasted thrushes. This, and its fondness for watery habitats, has resulted in the name "waterthrush." The Northern Waterthrush is often on the ground and seems to be in constant motion. Unlike many warblers, it walks rather than hops, bobbing its rump and tail up and down.

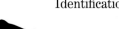

| | |
|---|---|
| Identification | 6". A sparrow-sized warbler that is olive-brown above and white below (including the flanks), with fairly heavy streaking. There is a yellowish eyebrow and a streaked throat. The similar Louisiana Waterthrush has a clear, white throat and a bold eye-line, as well as buff flanks. |
| Voice | A loud, rapid *chee-chee-chee, chew-chew-chew,* ending in a trill. Also, a slower *chip, chip, chip, chip.* |
| Habitat | Wooded swamps, lakeshores, and bogs; any woodland during migration. |
| Range | A northern bird; breeds from Alaska east through Canada, and south to Pennsylvania. |

## Louisiana Waterthrush  *Seiurus motacilla*

The Louisiana Waterthrush, like its close relative the Northern Waterthrush (see page 168), is an active, ground-dwelling species. This warbler's range is more southerly. In areas of their breeding range where both species occur, the Northern Waterthrush prefers still water, such as woodland ponds and swampy thickets, while the Louisiana Waterthrush favors swift-moving streams and, occasionally, southern riverine bottomlands.

Identification  6½". A sparrow-sized bird that is olive-brown above and white below, with fairly heavy streaking. It has a white eyebrow, buff flanks, and an unstreaked throat. The Northern Waterthrush has a yellowish eyebrow, white flanks, and a streaked throat.

Voice  Begins with 3 or 4 slurred, clear notes and ends in a brief jumble.

Habitat  Hillside brooks among dense woodlands, river swamps, and streams.

Range  From Minnesota and northeastern Texas east to New England and as far south as Georgia.

## Common Yellowthroat *Geothlypis trichas*

Like people, individual birds and birds from different geographical areas often have distinct accents or dialects. The Common Yellowthroat's song may vary from bird to bird or region to region. At times the basic phrase may sound like *witchity;* at other times it seems to be *witchy,* or even *witchery.* This species also has a loud, distinctive call note, an excellent aid to identifying an unseen bird in heavy cover.

Identification  4½–6". A sparrow-sized bird. Both sexes are olive above and yellow (varying regionally from bright to pale) below. Adult males are readily recognized by their bold, black face mask; females lack the mask but are normally identifiable by their olive and yellow plumage.

Voice  Variable. A loud, rolling *witchity-witchity-witchity,* often repeated; the call is a dry *tchet.*

Habitat  Moist woodlands, thickets, marshes, and swamps.

Range  From British Columbia east to Newfoundland and throughout the U.S.

## Sharp-tailed Sparrow *Ammodramus caudacutus*

Sparrows often get passed over by beginning birdwatchers as just so many "LBJs" (little brown jobs). Added to this reputation is the habit of some sparrows, the Sharp-tailed included, of skulking around in the undergrowth. While it is difficult to have a good look at a Sharp-tailed Sparrow, the ultimate reward is worthy of persistence. This little bird shows a subtle pattern and hues that are a true delight.

Identification    5½". Overall streaked above and buff below, with a gray central crown stripe and a gray neck. There is also an ocherous outline enclosing a gray ear patch. Western birds lack this distinct face pattern but are more richly ocherous and have white stripes on their backs.

Voice    A hissing, insectlike buzz.

Habitat    In the East, coastal marshes, particularly the drier grasses; inland, in grassy marshlands.

Range    Along the East and Gulf coasts, and from Alberta to Manitoba and south to North Dakota. Winters mainly along the Atlantic and Gulf coasts.

174

### Swamp Sparrow  *Melospiza georgiana*

Perhaps the best place to have a good look at the Swamp Sparrow is on its breeding grounds. Males typically choose a prominent perch from which to give their song, and this is almost the only time the bird remains in the open. Most often it stays undercover in dense reeds and grasses. During migration, Swamp Sparrows are regularly found in weed fields along with a variety of other sparrows.

Identification
5". Overall dark with a rusty cap (browner in winter) and wings and a gray nape area. Most young sparrows, the Swamp Sparrow included, are streaked below. An ill-defined chin patch may cause confusion with the somewhat similar White-throated Sparrow.

Voice
A series of soft notes loosely strung together: *chip-chip-chip-chip-chip;* or a soft, prolonged trill.

Habitat
Freshwater swamps and marshes; on migration, may be found with other sparrows in fields and brushy edges.

Range
From Alberta east to Newfoundland, south to the east-central U.S. Winters from the southern portion of the breeding range south.

176

## Red-winged Blackbird *Agelaius phoeniceus*

Perhaps one of our best-known wetland residents, the Red-winged Blackbird overwinters along the coasts and in large numbers southward. Their spring arrival is anticipated by birders in many parts of the country. Flocks of males arrive first, and their advertising song is frequently heard at this time. Females soon follow, and nesting proceeds through the summer. In fall, large flocks of blackbirds regularly canvass agricultural areas in search of unharvested seed. Winter flocks may consist of hundreds of thousands of birds.

**Identification** 7–9½". Males are a distinctive black with red shoulder patches; at times these colorful patches are well hidden. Females look more sparrowlike and are largely brown and heavily streaked. All adults have the long, pointed bill typical of blackbirds.

**Voice** A robust, ringing *konk-a-ree!*

**Habitat** Marshes, swamps, meadows, and pastures.

**Range** Widespread throughout North America, except parts of Alaska and the Far North.

## Yellow-headed Blackbird
*Xanthocephalus xanthocephalus*

The courtship song of the Yellow-headed Blackbird is almost as remarkable as the adult male's bright golden head and throat. An observer approaching a prairie pothole or wetland where a colony of these birds has settled will notice an unmusical, even cacophonous sound, a bit like someone is being strangled. Amid the noisy jockeying of the males, the females build their basketlike nests from various wetland grasses and reeds. Normally three or four eggs are laid, and the young leave the nest in three to four weeks.

| | |
|---|---|
| Identification | 8–11". Somewhat larger than the Red-winged Blackbird. The male is black with a yellow head, throat, and breast and a white wing patch. Females are brownish with duller and less extensive yellow. |
| Voice | Harsh, continuous *oka-wee-wee*, croaks, and *kruck* calls. |
| Habitat | Freshwater marshes, pastures, and grainfields. |
| Range | British Columbia to Manitoba and south to California, New Mexico, and Indiana. Winters in California and the extreme southwestern states. |

## Boat-tailed Grackle *Quiscalus major*

These noisy, large blackbirds seem almost ubiquitous within their range. Although most prevalent in and around coastal salt marshes, Boat-tailed Grackles are found inland throughout much of Florida. Their bulky, often conspicuous nests may be found in a variety of locations, including marshes, bushes, and numerous trees. Similar to the Great-tailed Grackle, found from Alabama westward, the Boat-tailed Grackle differs in having a duller-colored iris, ranging from dull yellow to brown.

Identification    Males, 16–17". Females, 12-13". Males are iridescent blue-black with long, pointed bills and keel-shaped tails. Females are strikingly different, being overall tan in color. Iris color ranges from yellow to brown.

Voice    A variety of guttural clicks, churs, and harsh *jeeh!* notes.

Habitat    Coastal marshes; in Florida, also inland lakes and streams.

Range    From Long Island south along the East and Gulf coasts, and in Florida.

# Parts of a Bird

crown

forehead

nape

back

chin

throat

secondaries

breast

tertials

flank

primaries

belly

tail feathers

undertail coverts

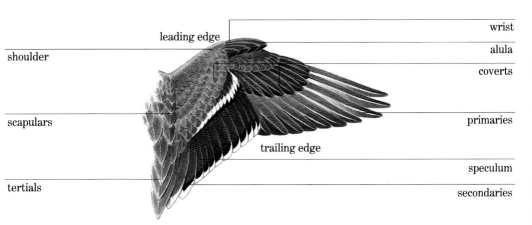

wrist

alula

coverts

leading edge

shoulder

primaries

scapulars

trailing edge

speculum

tertials

secondaries

185

# Glossary

**Accidental**
(See Vagrant.)

**Arthropod**
An invertebrate animal with jointed body and limbs, such as an insect, arachnid, or crustacean.

**Clutch**
A set of eggs laid by one bird.

**Coverts**
The small feathers covering the bases of other, usually larger, feathers. Coverts provide a smooth, aerodynamic surface.

**Crest**
A tuft of elongated feathers on the crown.

**Crown**
The uppermost surface of the head.

**Eye-ring**
A fleshy or feathered ring around the eye.

**Eye-stripe**
A stripe running horizontally from the base of the bill through the eye.

**Flight feathers**
The long feathers of the wing and tail used for flight. The flight feathers of the wing are comprised of primaries, secondaries, and tertials.

**Lore**
The area between the base of the bill and the eye.

**Mandible**
One of the two parts (upper and lower) of a bird's bill.

**Mantle**
The back and the upper surfaces of the wings.

**Mask**
An area of contrasting color on the front of the face and around the eyes.

## Morph
One of two or more distinct color types within the same species, occurring independently of age, sex, season, and geography. Also referred to as phase.

## Nape
The back of the head and the hindneck.

## Phase
(See Morph.)

## Race
(See Subspecies.)

## Rump
The lower back, just above the tail.

## Speculum
A distinctively colored area on the trailing edge of the wing, especially the iridescent patch on the secondaries of some ducks.

## Subspecies
A geographical population that is slightly different from other populations of the same species. Also called a race.

## Underparts
The lower surface of the body, including the chin, throat, breast, belly, sides, and undertail coverts.

## Vagrant
A bird that occurs outside its normal range. Also referred to as accidental.

## Wing bar
A bar of contrasting color on the upper wing coverts.

## Wing lining
A collective term for the coverts of the underwing.

## Wing stripe
A lengthwise stripe on the upper surface of the extended wing.

# Index

**A**

*Actitis macularia*, 120
*Aechmophorus occidentalis*, 30
*Agelaius phoeniceus*, 178
*Aix sponsa*, 66
*Ajaia ajaja*, 58
*Ammodramus caudacutus*, 174
*Anas acuta*, 74
*Anas crecca*, 68
*Anas cyanoptera*, 78
*Anas discors*, 76
*Anas platyrhynchos*, 72
*Anas rubripes*, 70
*Aramus guarauna*, 108
*Ardea herodias*, 40

**B**

Bittern, American, 36
Bittern, Least, 38
Blackbird, Red-winged, 178
Blackbird, Yellow-headed, 180
*Botaurus lentiginosus*, 36
*Branta canadensis*, 64
*Butorides virescens*, 48

**C**

*Calidris melanotos*, 124
*Calidris minutilla*, 122

*Casmerodius albus*, 42
*Ceryle alcyon*, 146
*Charadrius vociferus*, 114
*Chlidonias niger*, 144
*Chloroceryle americana*, 148
*Cinclus mexicanus*, 162
*Circus cyaneus*, 94
*Cistothorus palustris*, 160
Coot, American, 106
Cormorant, Double-crested, 34
*Corvus ossifragus*, 158
Crane, Sandhill, 110
Crane, Whooping, 112
Crow, Fish, 158
*Cygnus olor*, 62

**D**

*Dendroica petechia*, 164
Dipper, American, 162
Duck, American Black, 70
Duck, Ruddy, 84
Duck, Wood, 66

**E**

Eagle, Bald, 92
Egret, Great, 42
Egret, Snowy, 44
*Egretta caerulea*, 46

*Egretta thula*, 44
*Elanoides forficatus*, 88
*Empidonax trailii*, 150
*Eudocimus albus*, 54

F

Flycatcher, Willow, 150
*Fulica americana*, 106

G

*Gallinago gallinago*, 126
*Gallinula chloropus*, 104
Gallinule, Common. *See* Moorhen, Common.
Gallinule, Purple, 102
*Gavia immer*, 24
*Geothlypis trichas*, 172
Goose, Canada, 64
Grackle, Boat-tailed, 182
Grebe, Horned, 28
Grebe, Pied-billed, 26
Grebe, Western, 30
*Grus americana*, 112
*Grus canadensis*, 110
Gull, California, 136
Gull, Franklin's, 132
Gull, Ring-billed, 134

H

*Haliaeetus leucocephalus*, 92
Harrier, Northern, 94
Hawk, Marsh. *See* Harrier, Northern.
Heron, Black-crowned Night-, 50
Heron, Great Blue, 40
Heron, Green, 48
Heron, Little Blue, 46
Heron, Yellow-crowned Night-, 52

I

Ibis, White, 54
Ibis, White-faced, 56
*Ixobrychus exilis*, 38

K

Killdeer, 114
Kingfisher, Belted, 146
Kingfisher, Green, 148
Kiskadee, Great, 152
Kite, American Swallow-tailed, 88
Kite, Snail, 90

L

*Larus californicus*, 136
*Larus delawarensis*, 134
*Larus pipixcan*, 132
Limpkin, 108
Loon, Common, 24
*Lophodytes cucullatus*, 80

M

Mallard, 72
*Melospiza georgiana*, 176
Merganser, Common, 82
Merganser, Hooded, 80
*Mergus merganser*, 82
Moorhen, Common, 104
*Mycteria americana*, 60

N

*Nyctanassa violacea*, 52
*Nycticorax nycticorax*, 50

O

Osprey, 86
*Oxyura jamaicensis*, 84

P

*Pandion haliaetus*, 86
*Pelecanus erythrorhynchos*, 32

Pelican, American White, 32
*Phalacrocorax auritus,* 34
Phalarope, Wilson's, 130
*Phalaropus tricolor,* 130
Pintail, Northern, 74
*Pitangus sulphuratus,* 152
*Plegadis chihi,* 56
*Podiceps auritus,* 28
*Podilymbus podiceps,* 26
*Porphyrula martinica,* 102
*Porzana carolina,* 100
*Protonotaria citrea,* 166

**Q**
*Quiscalus major,* 182

**R**
Rail, King, 96
Rail, Virginia, 98
*Rallus elegans,* 96
*Rallus limicola,* 98
*Rostrhamus sociabilis,* 90

**S**
Sandpiper, Least, 122
Sandpiper, Pectoral, 124
Sandpiper, Solitary, 118

Sandpiper, Spotted, 120
*Scolopax minor,* 128
*Seiurus motacilla,* 170
*Seiurus noveboracensis,* 168
Snipe, Common, 126
Sora, 100
Sparrow, Sharp-tailed, 174
Sparrow, Swamp, 176
Spoonbill, Roseate, 58
*Stelgidopteryx serripennis,* 156
*Sterna antillarum,* 142
*Sterna caspia,* 138
*Sterna forsteri,* 140
Stork, Wood, 60
Swallow, Northern Rough-winged, 156
Swallow, Tree, 154
Swan, Mute, 62

**T**
*Tachycineta bicolor,* 154
Teal, Blue-winged, 76
Teal, Cinnamon, 78
Teal, Green-winged, 68
Tern, Black, 144
Tern, Caspian, 138
Tern, Forster's, 140

Tern, Least, 142
*Tringa flavipes,* 116
*Tringa solitaria,* 118

**W**
Warbler, Prothonotary, 166
Warbler, Yellow, 164
Waterthrush, Louisiana, 170
Waterthrush, Northern, 168
Woodcock, American, 128
Wren, Marsh, 160

**X**
*Xanthocephalus xanthocephalus,* 180

**Y**
Yellowlegs, Lesser, 116
Yellowthroat, Common, 172

# Credits

## Photographers

Ron Austing (95, 129, 157, 171, 177, 179)
Steve Bentsen (147, 153)
Sharon Cummings (22-23, 99, 107)
Rob Curtis/The Early Birder (97, 139, 143)

EMBINSKY PHOTO ASSOCIATES:
Dominique Braud (87)
Rod Planck (115)

Ron Farrar (37, 51)
Jeff Foott (55, 111, 163)
Chuck Gordon (29, 31, 33, 79, 125, 131, 133)
R.C. Kelley (69, 85, 181)
Harold Lindstrom (25, 35, 117, 119, 123, 167, 169)
Bates Littlehales (39, 47, 91, 109, 113, 183)
Barry W. Mansell (45)
Arthur & Elaine Morris/Birds As Art (41, 43, 59, 61, 65, 67, 73, 75, 105, 135, 137, 141, 151, 173)

PHOTO/NATS, INC.:
Cortez C. Austin, Jr. (Front Cover)

Rod Planck (27, 53, 71, 83, 159, 161)

ROOT RESOURCES:
Jim Flynn (81)
Ben Goldstein (103)

Ron Sanford (93)
Johann Schumacher Design (77)
Rob & Melissa Simpson (145, 165)
Tom J. Ulrich (57, 149)

VIREO:
Rob Curtis (175)
Brian Wheeler (89)

Mark F. Wallner (121, 127)
Larry West (3, 49)
Tim Zurowski (63, 101, 155)

Cover photograph: Snowy Egret by Cortez C. Austin, Jr/ PHOTO/NATS, INC.
Title page: Green Heron by Larry West
Spread (22-23): American Coot by Sharon Cummings

## Illustrators

Range maps by Paul Singer
Drawings by Barry Van Dusen (184-185)
Silhouette drawings by Douglas Pratt and Paul Singer

The photographers and illustrators hold copyrights to their works.

191

# Staff

This book was created by
Chanticleer Press.
All editorial inquiries should
be addressed to:
Chanticleer Press
568 Broadway, Suite #1005A
New York, NY 10012
(212) 941-1522

To purchase this book or other
National Audubon Society
illustrated nature books,
please contact:
Alfred A. Knopf, Inc.
201 East 50th Street
New York, NY 10022
(800) 733-3000

## Chanticleer Press Staff

Founding Publisher:
Paul Steiner
Publisher: Andrew Stewart
Managing Editor: Edie Locke
Production Manager:
Deirdre Duggan Ventry
Assistant to the Publisher:
Kelly Beekman
Text Editor: Carol M. Healy
Consultant: John Farrand, Jr.
Photo Editor: Lori J. Hogan
Designer: Sheila Ross
Research Assistant:
Debora Diggins

Original series design by
Massimo Vignelli.